THE
MINIATURES IN THE
GOSPELS OF ST AUGUSTINE

The Sandars Lectures in Bibliography

1948

THE
MINIATURES IN THE
GOSPELS OF ST AUGUSTINE

CORPUS CHRISTI COLLEGE MS. 286

BY

FRANCIS WORMALD

M.A., Litt.D., F.B.A., F.S.A.

PROFESSOR OF PALAEOGRAPHY
IN LONDON UNIVERSITY

CAMBRIDGE
AT THE UNIVERSITY PRESS
1954

CAMBRIDGE UNIVERSITY PRESS
Cambridge, New York, Melbourne, Madrid, Cape Town, Singapore,
São Paulo, Delhi, Dubai, Tokyo

Cambridge University Press
The Edinburgh Building, Cambridge CB2 8RU, UK

Published in the United States of America by Cambridge University Press, New York

www.cambridge.org
Information on this title: www.cambridge.org/9780521141536

A catalogue record for this publication is available from the British Library

ISBN 978-0-521-06868-0 Hardback
ISBN 978-0-521-14153-6 Paperback

Additional resources for this publication at www.cambridge.org/9780521141536

TO
THE MEMORY OF
F. SAXL

CONTENTS

THE PLATES

*Plates I and II are available for download in colour from www.cambridge.org/9780521141536

AUTHOR'S NOTE

THE ESSAY which precedes the plates here is an expanded version of the first of two lectures which I had the honour to deliver as Sandars Reader in Bibliography in the University of Cambridge for the year 1948. In discussing the miniatures in the Gospels of St Augustine I have purposely omitted any examination or discussion of the iconography of the scenes from the life of Christ and it is to be hoped that the plates in this book will stimulate students to pursue this side of the question. What is set down here is meant rather to form the basis for further study than a definitive edition of the miniatures. Owing to the kindness of the Master and Fellows of Corpus Christi College, Cambridge, I was able to make a careful examination of the MS., particularly the make-up of the gatherings, when it was being rebound during 1947 and 1948. The results of this examination have been incorporated into the description of the quires which will be found on p. 18. This study of the original MS. has also enabled me to make certain suggestions about the position and nature of some of the miniatures now lost from the MS.

It is my pleasant duty to record my thanks to various institutions and persons for their assistance: first to the University of Cambridge for honouring me as Sandars Reader, and secondly to the Master and Fellows of Corpus Christi College for allowing me constant access to their MS., particularly to Mr J. P. T. Bury, the College Librarian, for innumerable kindnesses. I am also grateful to the following for allowing me to reproduce objects and MSS. in their charge: the University Library, Cambridge, the Trustees of the British Museum, the Royal Library in Stockholm, the Landesmuseum in Karlsruhe, the Vatican Library, and Professor Gerke of Mainz. I am also most grateful to my friends at the Warburg Institute, London, particularly Dr Hugo Buchtal and Mr Patrick McGurk who have read the proofs. I owe much to discussions with Dr Otto Pächt, of Oriel College, Oxford and to the vigilance of my wife.

F. W.

JUNE 1953

THE MINIATURES IN
ST AUGUSTINE'S GOSPELS

AMONGST that remarkable group of MSS. collected by Matthew Parker, Archbishop of Canterbury, and presented by him to Corpus Christi College, Cambridge, the most venerable, not excepting the Anglo-Saxon Chronicle or the Chronica Majora of Matthew Paris, is the sixth-century MS. of the Gospels, MS. 286, formerly owned by St Augustine's Canterbury and sometimes associated with St Augustine the Apostle of the English.[1] There is nothing very improbable in this tradition. The main hand of the MS. is a sixth-century uncial and corrections in it show that it was in England by the end of the seventh or beginning of the eighth century.[2] It was certainly in St Augustine's Canterbury by the eleventh century when documents relating to that house were written into the MS. During the later Middle Ages it may well have been amongst the books which were placed with the relics on the high altar in the abbey church, and which are labelled in the fifteenth-century diagram of the sanctuary in Thomas of Elmham's chronicle, now in the library of Trinity Hall, Cambridge, 'libri missi a Gregorio ad Augustinum'.[3]

Palaeographers seem to agree that the MS. was written in Italy in the sixth century and Dr Lowe in his *Codices Latini Antiquiores* suggests that it was brought to England by the early missionaries. It will be remembered that Bede relates how St Gregory the Great sent books to St Augustine, and it is clear that Rome kept a close contact with the mission in those early days. It would, therefore, be quite natural for an illuminated Gospel-book to find its way into the possession of the new English foundation. In passing we may note that MSS. preserved in treasuries had a better chance of surviving pillage than those kept in the libraries.

---

[1] Cambridge, Corpus Christi College MS. 286. For a full description of the MS. see M. R. James, *A Descriptive Catalogue of the MSS. in the Library of Corpus Christi College, Cambridge*, vol. II (Cambridge, 1912), pp. 52 ff.; also E. A. Lowe, *Codices Latini Antiquiores*, vol. II (Oxford, 1935), no. 126 where an up-to-date bibliography will be found.

[2] Lowe, *loc. cit.*

[3] Cambridge, Trinity Hall MS. 1. For an engraving of the diagram see Dugdale, *Monasticon Anglicanum*, ed. Cayley, Ellis and Bandinel, I (London, 1817) between pp. 120 and 121. Six books are represented in this drawing. For the early MSS. at St Augustine's Canterbury, see M. R. James, *The Ancient Libraries of Canterbury and Dover* (Cambridge, 1903), pp. lxiii–lxxi. It is not possible to identify this MS. with any of the books mentioned by Elmham. On the other hand the absence of a press-mark in the MS. suggests perhaps that the book was kept in the Treasury and not amongst the Library books.

They were often regarded as relics and were, therefore, less accessible to the pre-datory or the careless. If a house was abandoned they also had a better chance of being carried away to safety.

According to Dr Lowe the St Augustine's Gospels is a pure Italian MS. and textually is related to an Italian Gospel-book of the seventh century, now in the Bodleian Library at Oxford, Bodleian MS. Auct. D. 11. 14.[1] The latter was in England by the eighth century when a liturgical reference to St Chad, bishop of Lichfield, was added in an Anglo-Saxon hand. There is no evidence to connect the Bodleian MS. with Canterbury, but there were connections, perhaps not very happy ones, between Canterbury and Lichfield in the second half of the eighth century, so the Oxford book may once have been at Canterbury. Both MSS., however, bear witness to the existence of Italian books in England during the eighth century.[2]

The Gospels of St Augustine, Cambridge, Corpus Christi MS. 286, is written in double columns in uncials, twenty-five lines to a column. Besides the two pages with miniatures there is no contemporary decoration, nor are there any ornamental initials. The only variety is that the first line or two of each Gospel is written in red and the opening words of some of the chapters are also written in red. As the MS. exists today only a small proportion of the original decoration remains. It is, how-ever, possible to make some suggestions on this scheme of decoration, though the conclusions submitted here can only be very tentative ones. Before discussing this, however, it is essential to give some idea of the surviving contents of the MS.

Owing to the loss of leaves the beginning of the MS. is incomplete. It is likely that before each Gospel there was the appropriate preface, followed by the chapter headings, followed by the Gospel. The arrangement might, therefore, have been: preface, chapter headings, Gospel. Before the Gospel of St Luke, which is the best preserved part of the MS., the arrangement is as follows: folio 124, end of St Mark, folio 124 verso, blank, folio 125 miniatures of scenes from the life of Christ arranged in squares (Plates I, III), folio 125 verso is blank, folio 126 has the preface to St Luke and on folios 127–9 are the chapter headings. On folio 129 verso is the famous miniature of St Luke seated under an arch in the bow of which is his symbol, the calf (Plates II, VII). On either side of the seated figure between the columns sup-porting the arch are small miniatures depicting scenes from the ministry of Christ. On folio 130 the text of the Gospel begins. The arrangement was, therefore, rect-angular miniature, preface, chapter headings, miniature of the evangelist, Gospel.

---

[1] Lowe, *CLA*, vol. II, no. 230.
[2] See F. M. Stenton, *Anglo-Saxon England* (Oxford, 1943), pp. 205, 206, 215, 216.

Although all the pictures once associated with the other Gospels have disappeared it is possible to say where some of them were placed and whether they were rectangular miniatures or arched like the miniature of St Luke. Owing to the loss of leaves at the beginning of the volume we cannot say with certainty whether a rectangular miniature was to be found before the preface to St Matthew. On the other hand on folio 3 (the first leaf of St Matthew) there are red stains which Dr M. R. James in his description of the MS. rightly diagnosed as offsets from a lost frontispiece. If this leaf is looked at in a good, but not a brilliant, light, it is possible to see the traces of two columns on the right as well as the bow of an arch. It seems reasonable, therefore, to conclude that this was a miniature of St Matthew seated under an arch with the symbol of the man above him. This conclusion is supported by the words 'Matheus Hominem' written in square capitals on the blank verso of folio 2 immediately after the end of the chapter headings. Dr Lowe in his description of the MS. suggests that these words were written on a page left blank for the reception of a miniature of the evangelist and his symbol. This suggestion seems unlikely since, as we have seen, a miniature of the evangelist and his symbol was on the verso of the following leaf which is now lost. There is, however, another possible explanation.

In the miniature of St Luke there is a band which runs across the miniature, forming an architrave. This bears the following inscription written in rustic capitals: 'Jura sacerdotii Lucas tenet ora iubenci'

These words come from lines 355–8 of the first Book of the *Carmen Paschale* of Sedulius and belong to a set of four lines describing the evangelists. Such verses are frequently found ornamenting miniatures of the evangelists in the Carolingian period. The complete four lines are as follows:

> 'Hoc Matthaeus agens, hominem generaliter implet.
> Marcus ut alta fremit vox per deserta leonis,
> Jura sacerdotis Lucas tenet ore juvenci.
> More volans aquilae, verbo petit astra Joannes.'[1]

On folio 207 verso at the top of the page opposite the beginning of St John the verse appropriate to that evangelist has been added in rustic capitals of the eighth century. The words 'Matheus Hominem' seem, therefore, to be taken from the lost inscription on the miniature of St Matthew and are a later addition made at the same time as the inscription from St John's verse, or possibly a little earlier.

---

[1] Migne, *Patrologia Latina*, vol. XIX, col. 591.

Before the Gospel of St Mark there is no indication of any rectangular miniature coming before the preface. In fact the arrangement of the gatherings seems to suggest that there never was one. The gatherings throughout the MS. are mainly of eight leaves, but the gathering in question, the thirteenth, was originally one of ten leaves, one leaf of which is now missing. This missing leaf contained the arched miniature of St Mark and came between folios 77 and 78. It has left a faint red ghost on folio 78 where something too may be seen of the drapery of the evangelist's robe. There is, moreover, at the top of folio 78 a drawing, made probably about A.D. 1100, of St Mark's symbol, the lion (Plate X). This is not a very competent work of art, but from its position on the page, as well as from other considerations to be discussed later, it appears to be a copy of the symbol which appeared on the lost miniature of St Mark. The date of this drawing is of some interest as it suggests that the lost miniature survived as late as the early twelfth century.

The arrangement of the miniatures for St John's gospel does not bear any relation to that of the other evangelists. From an offset on folio 206, it would seem that the arched miniature of the evangelist preceded the preface to the Gospel. A leaf is certainly missing between folios 205 and 206 and there are signs of an arched composition. There is, moreover, no indication of any miniature being placed before the beginning of the Gospel text, nor at this point is any loss of leaves indicated by the gathering. On the other hand, at the end of the Gospel on folio 265 verso, there are stains from the recto of a leaf which followed and which has now disappeared. These stains indicate a rectangular miniature divided up into squares and surrounded by a marbled border.

As it stands, therefore, the MS. had certainly four evangelist pictures under arches and two rectangular miniatures, one before St Luke, the second at the end of St John. There was apparently no such picture connected with St Mark and the portion of the MS. which might have contained it for St Matthew is missing. There are, however, other indications which are helpful. As we saw the composition of the gatherings was chiefly of eight leaves. Now the first twelve gatherings were numbered with a Roman numeral preceded by the letter Q placed in the right-hand bottom corner of the verso of the last leaf of each gathering. This numeration appears to be contemporary with the main hand of the text. Today the first surviving gathering number is Q iii on f. 10.[1] Therefore at least two whole gatherings

---

[1] There are signs that a renumeration of the gatherings took place in the thirteenth century by the fact that at the beginning of each gathering there is an erasure of a numeral in the right-hand bottom corner of the first recto of each gathering.

are missing and six leaves from the third gathering. Assuming that these gatherings were of eight leaves this means that twenty-two leaves are missing. The question is: What did these leaves contain? It is permissible only to make a few suggestions. These early Gospel-books were often prefixed by the letter of St Jerome to Damasus, a prologue to the Four Gospels, the letter of Eusebius to Carpianus relating to the Canon Tables and of course the Canon Tables themselves. This material should be followed by the preface to St Matthew.

All these contents might well account for the missing twenty-two leaves. The existence of a very large series of miniatures at the beginning of the MS. is not really very likely, unless we are to assume that the Canon Tables were not included in the quire numeration or that the miniatures themselves were excluded for the same reason. Yet even taking the most conservative estimate the cycle of scenes must have been a long and impressive one. In the rectangular miniature before St Luke there are twelve scenes. There were two such miniatures for certain, i.e. twenty-four scenes. In the miniature of St Luke there are six compartments, three on each side. Each compartment is divided into two separate scenes, so in this miniature twelve scenes are represented. We know that there were four evangelist miniatures with presumably forty-eight scenes. The complete certain score makes a cycle of 48+24 scenes or seventy-two scenes in all and there may well have been another twelve.

It has not been unprofitable to consider these minutiae. They indicate the existence of a very extensive cycle of Bible pictures which might well provide material for later copyists. Unfortunately, no copy of the MS. has survived, though certain elements may have exercised some influence on later MSS. Before comparing these miniatures with later works it is essential to sound a note of warning. It is impossible to prove that this individual Gospel-book provided the sole archetype for the later miniatures which are about to be discussed. A combination of circumstances does, however, establish a certain element of probability. The most profitable way of looking at the problem is to examine certain elements in the miniatures. It is convenient to take first the miniature of St Luke (Plates VII, XVIa).

The saint is shown seated on a chair in an alcove of which a certain element of perspective remains. On his knee is a book inscribed with the words 'Fuit homo missus a deo cui nomen erat Iohannes' (John i. 6). Behind his head hangs a garland of leaves. Both figure and alcove are framed by an edifice supported by four pillars, two on each side. On the architrave running above the pillars is the inscription from the *Carmen Paschale* of Sedulius written in rustic capitals. Above is a half circle composed of bands of decoration in the middle of which is the half-length symbol of St Luke, the winged calf holding a book between his forelegs (Plate XIV*a*). Between the two pillars on either side of the evangelist are scenes from the life of Christ (Plates VIII, IX). To each of these scenes a descriptive inscription has been added in insular uncials of the eighth century. The central form of the composition is a figure seated in an alcove in a round-headed edifice flanked by columns. Such compositions were known in illuminated MSS. as early as the middle of the fourth century.

It will be well to look at some early examples, for it will be seen that both the general composition and the figure have a very respectable ancestry. One of these ancestors must have been a MS. with compositions similar to those found in the famous fourth-century calendar of Philocalus (Plate XI).[1] The original MS. is lost, but later copies have survived; the most important being in the Vatican Library amongst the Barberini MSS. Another copy is in Vienna. If we look at two of the pages in this MS. it is clear that when certain elements in them are combined they form a composition similar to the architectural framework of the St Luke miniature in the Gospels of St Augustine. To take the top portion first. This is a lunette ornamented with a half-figure and supported by an architrave on which is an inscription in rustic capitals (Plate XIV*a*). The top portion of the page of the Philocalus calendar which contains the 'Natales Caesarum' shows a number of the same elements (Plate XI*a*). Fundamentally the construction is the same. Here is a half-figure, in this case of the Emperor, placed in a lunette edged with a broad patterned border. The lunette is supported by a broken architrave upon which are inscribed the words 'Natales Caesarum' in rustic capitals. The pages containing pictures of the planets have certain similarities in their top portions. The personification of the planets are shown standing under a round arch. On either side of the figures are two pillars enclosing a space filled in this case with text (Plate XI*b*). If these elements in the 'Natales Caesarum' page are combined with those of the planet pictures we obtain a composition which is fundamentally the same as that of the St Luke miniature.

There is, however, one element not found in the Philocalus calendar. In the St Augustine's Gospels, instead of text as in the planet picture, there is a series of scenes in rectangular panels placed vertically one on top of the other. Such an arrangement is not found in late antique book decoration, but it is found on certain pieces of sculpture. The late Professor Saxl noticed the similarity of arrangement

---

[1] See J. Strzygowski, *Die Calenderbilder des Chronographen vom Jahre 354* (Berlin, 1888); also Carl Nordenfalk, 'Der Kalender vom Jahre 354 und die lateinische Buchmalerei des IV Jahrhunderts' in *Göteborgs Kungl. Vetenskaps och Vitterhets-Samhälles Handlingar, Femte Foljden*, ser. A, Bd. 5, no. 2, 1936.

between the miniature in the St Augustine's Gospels and a stele of Mithras now in Karlsruhe (Plate XII*a*).[1] Here there is a big central figure surrounded by small scenes placed in rectangular panels. A similar arrangement can also be seen in the Heracles relief in the Naples Museum and on some early ivories.[2]

The figure of the evangelist also has forebears in late antique art. It has long been recognized that the portraits of the evangelists found in Gospel-books are derived from representations of the early poets and philosophers. In the case of St Luke a good parallel can be seen in a mosaic, probably of the third century, found at Susa in North Africa and now in the Museo del Bardo at Tunis (Plate XII*b*). This mosaic represents Virgil between Clio and Melpomene. The attitude of the head and of the right arm in this mosaic recalls very much St Luke, and the position of the legs in the mosaic, though reversed and awkwardly stylized in the miniature, bear many similarities. We are, therefore, in a position to say that the St Luke miniature is a composition whose elements are already found in late antique art of the third and fourth centuries.

No direct descendants have survived of the architectural arrangement of the St Luke miniature in either English or Continental illumination. There are of course many miniatures showing the evangelist sitting in an alcove with the symbols above in lunettes, but the stories placed between the columns are not found and this type of evangelist is usually writing or sharpening his pen and is not meditating. It is otherwise with the symbol of St Luke which has an interesting progeny which assists materially in the reconstruction of the appearance of the other evangelists and their symbols.

Before discussing the relationship between the evangelist symbols in St Augustine's Gospels and their possible descendants, something must be said about the varieties of symbols in use in England in the pre-Carolingian period. Broadly speaking there were two main types. The first represents the symbol as a complete animal, while the second shows only half the creature. Both forms were known in England by the end of the seventh century. The complete creatures are to be seen in the Book of Durrow,[3] the Majestas page of the Codex Amiatinus in Florence[4]

---

[1] Fritz Saxl, *Mithras, Typengeschichtliche Untersuchungen* (Berlin, 1931), p. 81, Pl. 15.

[2] For the Heracles relief see Adolph Goldschmidt, *An Early Manuscript of the Aesop Fables of Avianus and Related Manuscripts* (Princeton, 1947), Pl. XI, no. 13. For the ivories see the diptychs in the Duomo at Milan; the Museo Nazionale, Ravenna; Etschmiadzin; Bibliothèque Nationale, Paris. See W. F. Volbach, *Elfenbeinarbeiten der Spätantike u. des frühen Mittelalters* (Mainz, 1952), nos. 119, 125, 142, 145, of the fifth and sixth centuries.

[3] E. H. Zimmermann, *Vorkarolingische Miniaturen* (Berlin, 1916), Pls. 161, 162.

[4] *Ibid.* Pl. 222*.

and on the top of St Cuthbert's coffin, still preserved at Durham Cathedral.[1] The half-length symbols are to be found in the St Augustine's Gospels and in a very rudimentary form in a leaf now at the end of the Book of Durrow.[2] On the whole the complete creature either with or without a book seems to have been the more usual.

Both types were known on the Continent at an earlier date. In the transepts of San Vitale at Ravenna there are mosaics showing the evangelists seated in a rocky landscape. Over the head of each evangelist there is the appropriate complete creature. If such animals as those at San Vitale are taken by themselves they are to some extent the naturalistic predecessors of the stylized creatures of the Book of Durrow. The winged jumping creatures of the Lindisfarne Gospels[3] are perhaps more closely related to the sources of the Majestas miniature in the Codex Amiatinus, though the latter are without books,[4] and to the animals on St Cuthbert's coffin. The half-length symbol also can be found in late antique art. Besides the famous fourth-century mosaic at Santa Pudenziana in Rome, now very much restored, they may be seen on the mosaics in the baptistery of Soter in the cathedral in Naples,[5] and on the fifth-century wooden doors of the church of Santa Sabina in Rome. A more portable example is the late fifth-century ivory diptych now preserved in the treasury of Milan Cathedral (Plate XIII).[6]

St Luke's symbol in St Augustine's Gospels is of the family of half-length symbols, and from other evidence it is permissible to suggest that the remainder of the symbols were of the same type. By a fortunate chance there is in the British Museum, Royal MS. I E. VI, a fragment of a Bible, consisting now only of the Gospels, which once belonged to St Augustine's Canterbury (Plate XIV*b*).[7] It has been dated at the end of the eighth century. This MS. has at the beginning of St Luke a purple leaf decorated with an arch in the bow of which is the half-length symbol of St Luke which is extremely close to the symbol in St Augustine's Gospels. The colouring of this symbol also recalls the earlier MS., though a portion of it,

---

[1] E. Kitzinger, *The Coffin of St Cuthbert* (Oxford, 1950), Pl. 1.

[2] Zimmermann, *Vorkarolingische Miniaturen*, Pl. 165 *b*.   [3] *Ibid.* Pls. 223–6.

[4] An early example of the plain animal symbol is to be seen in the Valerianus Gospels in Munich, lat. 6224; see Zimmermann, *Vorkarolingische Miniaturen*, Pls. 5, 7.

[5] For the Soter mosaics, see M. van Berchem and E. Clouzot, *Mosaïques Chrétiennes du IVme au Xme Siècle* (Geneva, 1924), figs. 120, 121.

[6] Another sixth-century set of half-length symbols must have reached England at an early date with the illustrated copy of Sedulius' 'Carmen Paschale', of which a ninth-century copy of an insular copy exists today in the Musée Plantin at Antwerp; see W. Köhler in Paul Clemen's, *Belgische Kunstdenkmäler*, vol. I, pp. 7–11.

[7] See Lowe, *CLA*, vol. II, no. 214.

particularly the cloudy background, may be a later addition. This half-length symbol also recalls another eighth-century MS. once at Canterbury, the Codex Aureus in Stockholm.[1] We know from an inscription that it was bought from pagans, who had looted it, and restored to Canterbury. In this MS. there are two evangelist miniatures, St Matthew and St John, each accompanied by a half-length symbol (Plate XV).

Both Royal MS. I E. VI and the Codex Aureus appear to be copied from earlier continental models, and indeed, Canterbury seems to have made at least one other attempt to copy illuminations in earlier books. This is a picture of David harping, in a Psalter, now British Museum, Cotton MS. Vespasian A. I.[2] The Cotton MS. also belonged to St Augustine's Canterbury. The two miniatures in the Codex Aureus are unquestionably copies of earlier archetypes and should be compared with such MS. figures as those found in the sixth-century Codex Romanus in the Vatican (lat. 3867).[3] A small detail in the miniature of St Matthew in the Codex Aureus seems to connect this picture with the St Luke miniature in the Gospels of St Augustine. On either side of St Luke small leafy plants are growing and the same plants appear in a stylized form in the Stockholm figure of St Matthew (Plate XVI).[4] In fact the miniature in the Codex Aureus contains three elements which are also found in the Gospels of St Augustine: in both the evangelist is seen meditating, both have half-length symbols and in both small plants grow up on either side of the figure of the evangelist.

There seems, therefore, to be a case for arguing that in both Royal MS. I E. VI and the Codex Aureus there are certain connexions with the Gospels of St Augustine. This seems particularly true of the evangelist symbols which can consequently be used to assist in an attempt to discover what the missing symbols were like. In this attempt another MS., the ninth-century Book of Cerne, now in the University Library at Cambridge, can be of great assistance.[5] This MS. was probably written in Mercia in the first half of the ninth century.

Generally speaking the evangelist symbols in the Book of Cerne resemble the great barbaric creatures such as are found in the Echternach Gospels in Paris, British

[1] Zimmermann, *Vorkarolingische Miniaturen*, Pls. 282, 283; see also C. Nordenfalk in *Nordisk Tidskrift für Bok- och Biblioteksväsen*, vol. XXXVIII (1951), pp. 145–55.

[2] *Ibid*. Pl. 286a.

[3] See F. Saxl and R. Wittkower, *British Art and the Mediterranean* (Oxford, 1948), Pl. 14, no. 4.

[4] It should be noted that highly stylized plants grow up on either side of the figures of the evangelists in the eighth-century Gospels in the Vatican Library, Barberini lat. 570; see Zimmermann, *Vorkarolingische Miniaturen*, Pls. 313, 314.

[5] See Zimmermann, *tom. cit.* Pls. 295, 296.

Museum Cotton MS. Otho C. v and Cambridge, Corpus Christi MS. 197.[1] They are not quite so stylized as these creatures. On the other hand they are far more barbaric than the Canterbury MSS. which have just been mentioned. Unlike those in the Echternach Gospels they clutch books in a manner which recalls the half-length symbols. Moreover, their fronts and their backs are most awkwardly integrated. They appear in fact to be hybrids, and their foreparts derived from half-length symbols like the St Augustine's Gospels and the Codex Aureus; while their hindquarters belong really to full-length animals such as those of the Book of Durrow and the Echternach group. This curious mixture can be easily detected if the symbol of St Luke in the Book of Cerne (Plate XVIII) is compared with that of the Book of Durrow. In the former the front of the creature does not belong to the back, and, if the head and book are looked at independently of the hindquarters, they will be seen to bear a great similarity to the symbol in St Augustine's Gospels. This can be observed in the pose of the head and the arrangement of the forelegs round the book.

A like comparison can be made between the symbols of St Mark in St Augustine's Gospels and the Book of Cerne (Plates X, XVII). Unfortunately, in the former the symbol is a later copy. Nevertheless, there is a connexion between the two. Some have considered that the St Mark's symbol in the Gospels of St Augustine has the face of a man and should therefore be placed in the entirely distinct category of anthropomorphic symbols. In the Book of Cerne this is clearly not so, and any human appearance the creature may have can be attributed to the poorness of the copy. This symbol is not far removed from the lion in the Book of Cerne and in both can be observed a certain stylization of the original. A similar comparison can be made between the representations of the eagle of St John in the Codex Aureus and the Book of Cerne (Plates XVb, XIX). Once again the heads and upper portions of the two creatures are very similar, sufficiently like to suggest a close relationship. St Matthew's angel is less similar in the two MSS., but it must be remembered that in the Book of Cerne this figure has been a good deal stylized.

The connexion between the symbols in the Book of Cerne, Royal MS. IE. VI, the Codex Aureus in Stockholm and the Gospels of St Augustine is sufficiently close to merit the suggestion that these MSS. represent the type of symbol in use at Canterbury during the pre-Carolingian period. It is tempting to suggest that they all derive from the Gospels of St Augustine, but it would be rash to insist on this. Nevertheless, it seems probable that the lost symbols in the Corpus MS. resembled the later books and that the evangelists were of a type similar to those in the Codex

[1] Zimmermann, *tom. cit.* Pls. 255, 256, 259, 266e.

Aureus. It would be, however, quite unjustifiable to say that these figures were copied from St Augustine's Gospels. This would only be possible if it could be assumed that the colours used in the lost pages were very different from the two which have survived.[1] The style of the miniatures in the Codex Aureus suggests that its archetype may have been nearer to the Codex Romanus.

Having examined certain aspects of the St Luke miniature we can pass to the rectangular miniature which stands before the preface to St Luke's Gospel on folio 125 (Plate III). This miniature consists of a rectangular frame, painted to represent marble, surrounding twelve rectangular panels arranged in four rows of three panels. Each of these inner panels is bordered in red and contains scenes from the life of Christ. Such pages are known in early MSS. as for instance the Vatican Virgil of the fourth century, the Quedlinburg Itala[2] fragments and the sixth-century Dioscorides MS. in Vienna.[3] Such arrangements survive in later MSS.[4] The marbled border is far more rare and we shall have occasion to refer to it later in another connexion.

It is not the purpose of this essay to discuss the iconography of the scenes represented in these miniatures, but certain features must be examined. First, it is permissible to make a general distinction between the scenes represented in the two miniatures. On the rectangular page the scenes are concerned with occurrences during the Passion, beginning with the Entry to Jerusalem on Palm Sunday and ending with Simon of Cyrene being made to bear the cross of the Lord. The small scenes on either side of St Luke in the other miniature are devoted to the ministry, particularly miracles and parables. This distinction may be due to a division between the important series of scenes relating the Passion of Christ and a series more directly concerned with the ministry and thaumaturgical acts of our Lord.[5] The choice of scenes in the rectangular miniature seems to imply the necessity of at least two other similar pages, one coming earlier in the MS. and illustrating the birth and early life

[1] In the Codex Aureus it is clear that the figures of the evangelists have undergone serious modifications, and in the miniature of St John two roundels of purely 'insular' ornament have been introduced into the decoration.

[2] H. Degering and A. Boeckler, *Die Quedlinberger Italafragmente* (Berlin, 1932).

[3] See Kurt Weitzmann, *Illustrations in Roll and Codex* (Princeton, 1947), fig. 78.

[4] E.g. in the ninth-century MS. of St Gregory Nazianzen in Paris, Bibl. Nat. grec 510 (see H. Omont, *Miniatures des plus anciens MSS. grecs de la Bibliothèque Nationale du VIᵐᵉ au XIVᵐᵉ Siècle* (Paris, 1929), Pls. XXII, XLVIII); also twelfth-century leaves of an English MS. now in the British Museum, the Victoria and Albert Museum and New York, Pierpont Morgan Library (see *Walpole Society*, vol. XXV); the leaves preceding the copy of the Utrecht Psalter in Paris Bibl. Nat. lat. 8846. An early thirteenth-century English example is in Trinity College Cambridge MS. B. 11. 4. Numerous Continental examples could doubtless be cited.

[5] See André Grabar, *Martyrium, Recherches sur le Culte des Reliques et l'Art Chrétien Antique*, vol. II (Paris, 1946), pp. 236–9.

of Christ, the other coming later and completing the cycle of the Passion. The existence of the latter is certain, since a page of this kind is known to have existed at the end of St John's Gospel.

It is clear that even at this early date the position of some of the scenes had already become disturbed. In the surviving rectangular miniature which represents scenes from the Passion, the Raising of Lazarus has intruded into the second row. The following scene of the Washing of the Feet is also out of place and strictly should follow the Last Supper and precede the Agony in the Garden which is the last scene of the first row. The intrusion of the Lazarus scene cannot be explained by the fact that the portion of St John's Gospel which tells this story is used on the Friday before Passion Sunday, but a suggestion can be made about the position of the Washing of the Feet.

Both in the Gospels and in the monuments the Last Supper and the Washing of the Feet are closely connected. The same is true of St Augustine's Gospels, because the Last Supper is placed immediately above the Washing of the Feet. It is likely, therefore, that these two scenes were together in the archetype of the miniature and that the two miniatures do in fact represent what was once a single composition.[1] If this is so, the strange appearance of the lamp in the Washing of the Feet scene could easily be explained, for it would belong to the Last Supper scene and form part of the usual East Christian iconography of that scene.[2] The system of breaking up the scenes used in the miniatures also tends to support this suggestion. Normally where two scenes appear within the same rectangular frame they are separated from each other by a wavy line giving a somewhat hilly appearance. Such a device may be seen in the miniature of the Agony in the Garden where in the top portion Christ is seen praying on the Mount of Olives, while below he is addressing his sleeping disciples with the words 'Sleep on now and take your rest'. If such a line of demarcation were stylized it might well become just a straight line dividing the original rectangular miniature into two rectangular scenes.

This system of stylizing the division lines of the scenes within a rectangular frame introduces the question of the relationship between the miniatures in St Augustine's Gospels to four leaves painted with Scriptural scenes in England in the twelfth century. These leaves which are now preserved in the British Museum, the Victoria

---

[1] For a twelfth-century example which bears certain iconographical resemblances, see Oxford, Bodleian MS. Douce 293, f. 11, reproduced in Bodleian Library, *Scenes from the Life of Christ in English Manuscripts* (Bodleian Picture Book No. 5, Oxford, 1951), Pl. 14.

[2] See Gabriel Millet, *Recherches sur l'Iconographie de l'Evangile* (Paris, 1916), pp. 310, 311, for examples of the occurrence of the lamp in the scene of the Washing of the Feet.

and Albert Museum, London, and the Pierpont Morgan Library in New York, were discussed by Dr M. R. James in an article published after his death in the annual volume of the Walpole Society.[1] In more than one respect the arrangement of the scenes on these leaves invites comparison with the arrangement in St Augustine's Gospels. First, the illustrations are placed in rectangular frames, six on a page. Secondly, in some cases the scenes are divided into narrower panels which resemble the scenes flanking the figure of St Luke. But even more striking is the way in which some of the scenes are still further divided into small scenes of irregular size, as in the case of the section devoted to the parable of the Prodigal Son.[2] Such divisions might well derive from a stylization of the system found in St Augustine's Gospels.

In his discussion of these leaves Dr James drew attention to the occurrence of the rare illustration of the parable found in Luke ix. 58: 'Foxes have holes, and the birds of the air have nests, but the Son of Man hath not where to lay his head.'[3] In the miniature of St Luke, the third scene on the right, there is a scene with this inscription: 'Ihesus dixit vulpes fossa habent.' Without this inscription it would be quite impossible to say that the scene referred to Luke ix. 58, for it merely represents Christ addressing three persons. In the twelfth-century leaf, however, the scene is quite easily identifiable, for the top portion of the miniature shows the foxes in their holes and the birds in their nests. In the lower portion Christ with six disciples points to the scene above. The identification of the scene in St Augustine's Gospels depends, therefore, entirely on the inscription which, according to the greatest living authority on these matters, is an addition made by an eighth-century hand. The only conclusion that can be drawn is that the writer of the inscriptions had access to a large set of illustrations from which he could make an attempt to label the scenes which were originally not identified in the Gospels of St Augustine. If, as has been suggested, the twelfth-century leaves do represent a much earlier set of illustrations it may be that this early set provided the eighth-century Englishman with a means of annotating the St Augustine's Gospels.

In an important study of a series of Old Testament pictures, now in the Walters Art Gallery at Baltimore, Dr Hanns Swarzenski suggests in passing that it is possible that the miniatures in St Augustine's Gospels are English copies made in the eighth century of Late Antique miniatures which had found their way into England.[4] This

---

[1] *Walpole Society*, vol. xxv (1937), pp. 1–23, Pls. I–VIII.
[2] *Ibid.* Pl. v (Pierpont Morgan MS. 521), the last rectangle of the lowest row.   [3] *Ibid.* p. 20.
[4] H. Swarzenski, 'Unknown Bible Pictures by W. de Brailes' in *The Journal of the Walters Art Gallery*, vol. I (Baltimore, 1938), pp. 55–69 (particularly pp. 67, 69).

is in some ways an attractive theory. It would easily explain why the inscriptions look so much at one with the miniatures. The dislocation and truncation of the scenes might also be explained as the aberrations of artists who misunderstood their archetypes. On the other hand the two leaves on which the miniatures are painted are leaves which have always belonged to the book and are still conjoint with their opposite numbers in the gathering. There can, therefore, be no question of the leaves being inserted at a later date. Of course the leaves may have been left blank waiting for the paintings to be added, but there is really no evidence that they ever were.

Apart from these considerations both the style and colour of the miniatures in St Augustine's Gospels do not resemble those miniatures painted in England in the eighth century which are copied from earlier Continental models. Both the David miniature in British Museum, Cotton MS. Vespasian A. I and the evangelists in the Codex Aureus in Stockholm show a degree of stylization far more drastic than anything to be seen in the Gospels. Moreover, the colour in the two English MSS. is quite different, being far heavier. Besides in both the Vespasian Psalter and the Stockholm Gospels insular elements have crept into the ornament. Even St Luke's symbol in B.M. Royal MS. IE. VI shows considerable transformation, particularly in the hardening of the outline, which at once proclaims it an insular copy. Until much more precise evidence is forthcoming it is difficult to avoid considering the two miniatures in St Augustine's Gospels as anything but part of the original decoration of the MS. and of the sixth century.

If these two miniatures are of the sixth century, can they be related to any other miniatures? Unfortunately, no miniatures of this date survive from the Latin West. Compared with the paintings in the fifth-century Virgil, the Codex Romanus in the Vatican, they show a greater degree of stylization. These stylizing tendencies in the Gospels of St Augustine are very important and characteristic. They can be seen in a variety of forms. In the draperies the folds are represented by calligraphic lines which avoid any attempt at modelling. Such stylization can be clearly seen in the robe of St Luke or in a much more exaggerated form in the treatment of the folds on Christ's thigh in the scene of the Entry into Jerusalem where the lines indicating folds have been reduced to a trefoil pattern (Plate IV1). This process of reduction may also be seen in the architecture in the scenes of the Entry into Jerusalem and the Raising of Lazarus (Plate IV4). The transformation of the once illusionistic landscape is also quite remarkable. This is achieved by reducing hills into a series of conventionally rendered billows of a different colour (Plate I). There is no attempt at gradations of colour which is the normal feature of illusionistic painting: even the Codex Romanus still retains a vestige of this. In this conventionally rendered landscape trees have become arabesques and grasses are laid against the landscape like the veins of a leaf (Plates V 8, VI 12).

If material cannot be found amongst sixth-century MSS. it is legitimate to look amongst later copies of sixth-century originals to see if any of them can be compared with the miniatures in the Gospels of St Augustine. Adolph Goldschmidt in his charming book on the MS. of the Aesop Fables of Avianus has discussed the illustrations in this MS., which is in the Bibliothèque Nationale in Paris; and compared them with an Apocalypse now part of the same MS.[1] He shows that both are Carolingian copies of sixth-century originals. To these two may be added the Apocalypses of Trier and Cambrai which seem to be copies of a sixth-century MS.[2] If these Carolingian copies can be regarded as representing not only the iconography, but also the style of their archetypes, all show a stage of stylization approximate to that in the miniatures in the Gospels of St Augustine. In all these MSS. there is a similar reduction in the calligraphic treatment of the folds, though the Avianus and the Paris Apocalypse are more exaggerated in this respect. Such details as the small twig-like extensions at the sides of the folds in the frontispiece of the Avianus recall the curious leaf-like arrangement of the folds on the thigh of Christ in the Entry to Jerusalem picture.[3] This reduction to terms of pattern can also be observed in the treatment of the folds on the lap of the figure of Avianus in this frontispiece. The arrangement of the legs in the figure of Augustus in this miniature appears rather like a maladroit version of that in the figure of St Luke.

It is, however, in the general appearance of the colour and form that the similarity between these Carolingian copies and the Gospels of St Augustine is most convincing. In the Trier and Cambrai Apocalypses we find the same use of pale blue, terra-cotta and yellow ochre, and the short figures with rather large heads and staring eyes should be compared, and though less linear in treatment the Cambrai Apocalypse reminds one of the St Augustine's miniatures. In making this stylistic comparison there may be some objection to the use of later MSS., but bearing in mind that they are later copies, both the Trier and Cambrai Apocalypses show

---

[1] A. Goldschmidt, *An Early MS. of the Aesop Fables*. The number of the MS. is Paris, Bibl. Nat. lat. nouv. acq. 1132.

[2] For reproductions of Cambrai MS. 386, see H. Omont, 'Manuscrits Illustrés de l'Apocalypse aux IXᵉ et Xᵉ Siècles' in *Bulletin de la Société Française de Reproductions de MSS. à Peintures*, 6 année (Paris, 1922), Pls. XXIX–XXXI. For Trier, Stadtbibliothek MS. 31, see A. Boinet, *La Miniature Carolingienne* (Paris, 1913), Pls. CLIII–CLV, and A. Goldschmidt, *Die Deutsche Buchmalerei*, vol. 1 (Florence, 1928), Pl. 54.

[3] Goldschmidt, *An Early MS. of the Aesop Fables*, Pl. 1 and this book Pl. IV 1.

sufficient similarity to allow one some idea of the appearance of the original. At the same time there are certain details in these Carolingian copies which are absent in the Cambridge miniatures. In particular Goldschmidt noticed one detail which is never found in the Gospels of St Augustine. This is a device whereby the hem of the back of a garment is seen from the front as a series of frills which are lower than the front hem.[1] Actually this hem does not appear in the Cambrai or Trier Apocalypses in its scalloped form, but it appears as a line drawn lower than the line of the front hem giving the impression that the garment is longer at the back than at the front.

On this slight evidence the miniatures in the Gospels of St Augustine cannot be considered as examples of the style of the originals of either the Avianus or of the two Apocalypses, but they can be said to belong to the same stage of late antique art. It is, moreover, impossible to localize them in any given centre in Western Europe. Goldschmidt suggested that the original of the Avianus MS. came from Vienne, but the origin of the two Apocalypses still remains a mystery. On palaeographical grounds the Gospels of St Augustine have been assigned to Italy and it may well be that they are examples of some provincial Italian centre. Too little is known of this period, but in considering the origins the Syrian features in the iconography should be taken into account. It is to be hoped that this study may stimulate further and more conclusive investigations.

[1] Goldschmidt, *An Early MS. of the Aesop Fables*, p. 23.

DESCRIPTION OF THE QUIRES IN C.C.C. MS. 286

Present quire numeration	Ancient quire numeration	Present foliation	Number of leaves in gatherings	Notes whether the leaves are still conjoint
1	iii = Q. iii	ff. 1, 2	2, probably 8; lacks 1–5, 8	Neither two leaves are conjoint
2	iv = Q. iiii	ff. 3–10	8 leaves	3 and 10 no longer conjoint; 4–9, 5–8, 6–7
3	v = Q. v	ff. 11–18	8 leaves	11 and 18 no longer conjoint; 12–17, 13–16, 14–15
4	vi = Q. vi	ff. 19–26	8 leaves	19 and 26 no longer conjoint; 20–5, 21–4, 22–3
5	vii = Q. vii	ff. 27–34	8 leaves	27 and 34 no longer conjoint; 28–33, 29–32, 30–1
6	viii = Q. viii	ff. 35–42	8 leaves	35–42, 36–41, 37–40, 38–9
7	ix = Q. viiii	ff. 43–50	8 leaves	43–50, 44–9, 45–8, 46–7
8	x = Q. x	ff. 51–8	8 leaves	51 and 58 no longer conjoint; 52–7, 53–6, 54–5
9	xi = Q. xi	ff. 59–66	8 leaves	59 and 66 no longer conjoint; 60–5, 61–4, 62–3
10	xii = Q. xii	ff. 67–74	8 leaves	67 and 74 no longer conjoint; 68–73, 69–72, 70–1
11	xiii	ff. 75–83	9, originally 10; lacks no. 4	75 and 83 no longer conjoint; 76–82, 77–81, 78–9, 80 single leaf owing to loss of no. 4 between ff. 77 and 78
12	xiiii	ff. 84–91	8 leaves	84 and 91 no longer conjoint; 85–90, 86–9, 87–8
13	[xv]	ff. 92–9	8 leaves	92 and 99 no longer conjoint; 93–8, 94–7, 95–6
14	[xvi]	ff. 100–7	8	100–7, 101–6, 102–5, 103–4
15	xvii	ff. 108–15	8	108 and 115 no longer conjoint; 109–14, 110–13, 111–12
16	[xviii]	ff. 116–23	8	116–23, 117–22, 118–21, 119–20
17	[xix]	ff. 124–30	7, originally 8; lacks no. 8	124, single owing to loss of leaf after 130, 125–30, 126–9, 127–8
18	[xx]	ff. 131–8	8	131 and 138 no longer conjoint; 132–7, 133–6, 134–6
19	[xxi]	ff. 139–46	8	139–46, 140–5, 141–4, 142–3
20	xxii	ff. 147–54	8	147–54, 148–53, 149–52, 150–1
21	xxiii	ff. 155–62	8	155–62, 156–61, 157–60, 158–9
22	[xxiiii]	ff. 163–70	8	163–70, 164–9, 165–8, 166–7
23	[xxv]	ff. 171–8	8	171–8, 172–7, 173–6, 174–5
24	[xxvi]	ff. 179–86	8	179–86, 180–5, 181–4, 182–3
25	[xxvii]	ff. 187–94	8	187–94, 188–93, 189–92, 190–1
26	[xxviii]	ff. 195–202	8	195–202, 196–201, 197–200, 198–9
27	[xxix]	ff. 203–5	3, originally 4; lacks no. 4	203, single owing to the loss of a leaf after 205, 204–5
28	[xxx]	ff. 206–13	8	206–13, 207–12, 208–11, 209–10
29	[xxxi]	ff. 214–21	8	214–21, 215–20, 216–19, 217–18
30	[xxxii]	ff. 222–9	8	222–9, 223–8, 224–7, 225–6
31	[xxxiii]	ff. 230–7	8	230–7, 231–6, 232–5, 233–4
32	[xxxiv]	ff. 238–45	8	238 and 245 no longer conjoint; 239–44, 240–3, 241–2
33	[xxxv]	ff. 246–53	8	246–53, 247–52, 248–51, 249–50
34	[xxxvi]	ff. 254–61	8	254–61, 255–60, 256–9, 257–8
35	[xxxvii]	ff. 262–5	4	262 and 265 no longer conjoint; 263–4

Folio 265 was followed by at least one leaf which was illuminated, and was probably of the rectangular type found on folio 125. The offset from this illumination can be seen on folio 265 b.

THE PLATES

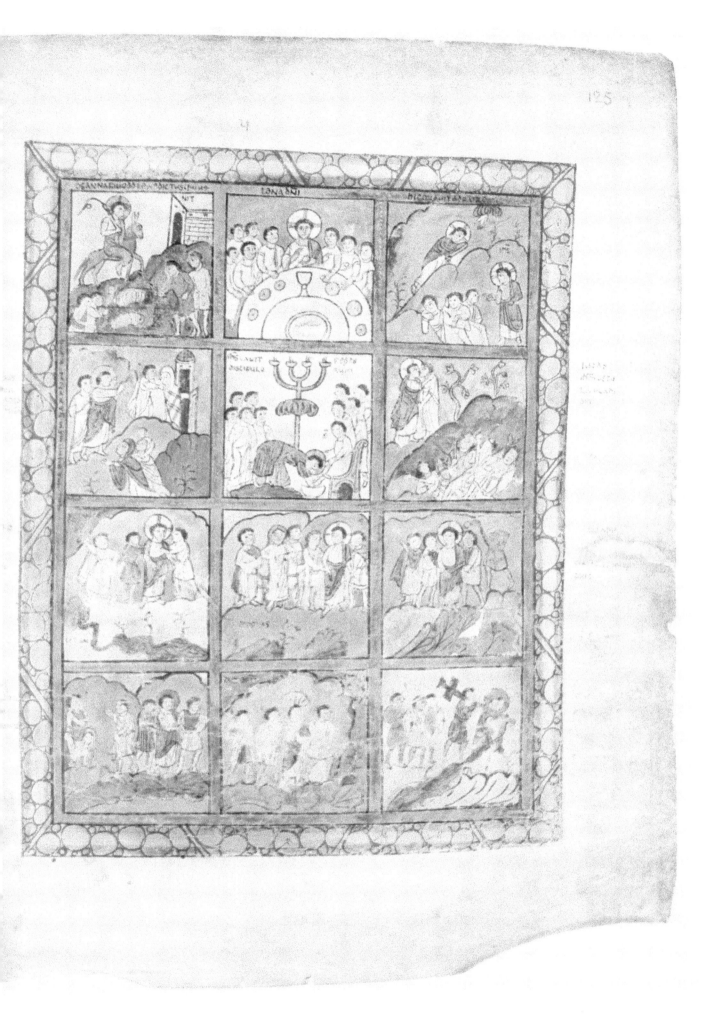

PLATE I

CAMBRIDGE, CORPUS CHRISTI COLLEGE MS. 286, f. 125

PLATE II

CAMBRIDGE, CORPUS CHRISTI COLLEGE MS. 286, f. 129b

PLATE III

CAMBRIDGE, CORPUS CHRISTI COLLEGE MS. 286, f. 125

Scenes from the life of Christ. Original size

PLATE IV

1. THE ENTRY INTO JERUSALEM

OSANNAFILIODDBENEDICTUSQUIUE | NIT

OSANNA FILIO DAVID BENEDICTUS QUI VENIT written above. Christ beardless holding a scourge in his right hand, riding on an ass towards the city gate. Below on *l.* two figures strewing garments which are placed between them and two figures on *r.*, one holding a palm branch. See G. Millet, *Iconographie de l'Evangile*, pp. 264, 270. (Matt. xxi. 9.)

2. THE LAST SUPPER

CENA DÑI

CENA DOMINI. Christ seated in the middle of a group of eight disciples seated at a round table. Before him is the cup and in the centre of the table the paschal lamb of the Passover. Before the disciples are placed breads. Christ holds the bread in his left hand blessing with the right. It should be noted that the disciples on his left repeat his gesture. See Millet, *op. cit.* pp. 300, 301, 308.

3. THE AGONY IN THE GARDEN

hICORAUITADPATREM

HIC ORAVIT AD PATREM. Above Christ prostrate in prayer. A hand descends from the clouds. Below Christ, ihs written above, addresses the three sleeping disciples.

4. THE RAISING OF LAZARUS

MARIA | ETMAR | THAROÇA | BANTDÑM

MARIA ET MARTHA ROGABANT DOMINUM written in the left-hand margin of the page. In the left-hand border of the miniature: Ihs LAZARUM SUSCITAUIT (IESUS LAZARUM SUSCITAVIT). Above Christ with two disciples calls Lazarus from a tower-like tomb. One disciple runs forward to support Lazarus. Below are Martha and Mary praying. (John xi.)

PLATE IV
CAMBRIDGE, CORPUS CHRISTI COLLEGE MS. 286, f. 125
Enlarged details

PLATE V

5. THE WASHING OF THE FEET

ihsLauit pedes | discipulo rum

IESUS LAVIT PEDES DISCIPULORUM. Christ girded with a towel bends down and takes in his hands the feet of St Peter which are placed in a basin. St Peter sits in a chair and bends forward with arms outstretched towards Christ. There are nine disciples standing, five on the left and four on the right. In the middle is a standard lamp with four lights burning. As has been suggested above this lamp probably originally belonged to a Last Supper scene which was combined with the Washing of the Feet. See Millet, *op. cit.* p. 311.

6. THE BETRAYAL AND THE STUPEFACTION OF THE SOLDIERS

Iudas | ihm oscu | Lotradi | dit

IUDAS IESUM OSCULO TRADIDIT written in the right-hand margin. The scene is divided into two by a billowing hill. In the top portion Christ is kissed by Judas who comes from the right. Below four soldiers with staves fall to the ground (cf. John xviii. 6). See Millet, *op. cit.* pp. 329, 330.

7. THE TAKING OF CHRIST

Iniece | runt | manus | inihm

INIECERUNT MANUS IN IESUM (cf. Matt. xxvi. 50) written in the left margin. Christ seized by two men. On the left a figure labelled petrus (St Peter) advances brandishing a sword. Below a river running from left to right labelled cedron (cf. John xviii. 1).

8. CHRIST BEFORE CAIAPHAS

There is no inscription except the name caiphas written on the ground to the left. On the left the High Priest between two men rises from a square throne tearing his garments. On the right Christ seized by two men.

PLATE V
CAMBRIDGE, CORPUS CHRISTI COLLEGE MS. 286, f. 125
Enlarged details

PLATE VI

9. THE BUFFETING OF CHRIST

ḥıcaᴌapıs | çaeᴆeꞚạɴᴛ | euᴍ eᴛpu | çɴıs

HIC ALAPIS CAEDEBANT EUM ET PUGNIS (cf. Mark xiv. 65) written in the right margin. Christ held by the wrists by two men on either side of whom are other men with right hands raised to strike. The one on the right has his fist clenched.

10. PILATE WASHES HIS HANDS

pıᴌạᴛus | ᴌauıᴛ | ᴍaɴus | suas

PILATUS LAVIT MANUS SUAS written in the left-hand margin. On the left Pilate seated holding out his hands over which a servant pours water from a long-handled ladle-like utensil. A rather similar object, though with a shorter handle, is used to receive the water poured from a jug, in the representation of this scene on the fourth-century ivory box in the Museo Cristiano at Brescia; see the excellent photographs reproduced in *Atlantis*, Heft 2 (1949), p. 88. On the right Christ led away by two men.

11. CHRIST LED OUT TO BE CRUCIFIED

ᴆuxeɴᴛ̄ uᴛcꞃu | cıꝑç | eʀ

DUXERUNT UT CRUCIFIGERENT (cf. Matt. xxvii. 31) written above. Christ led by one soldier and followed by two others bearing swords (?) and shields. Christ's halo is unusual, being provided with rays.

12. SIMON OF CYRENE BEARS THE CROSS

There are vestiges of an inscription in the right-hand margin beginning with an H (? HIC), but the words are almost entirely obliterated. Christ walks on the right bearing a cross with a long shaft. Simon of Cyrene walks behind supporting the cross on his right shoulder. Three soldiers walk behind. All bear shields. One carries a spear, another a short sword.

PLATE VI

CAMBRIDGE, CORPUS CHRISTI COLLEGE MS. 286, f. 125
Enlarged details

PLATE VII

CAMBRIDGE, CORPUS CHRISTI COLLEGE MS. 286, f. 129b

St Luke the Evangelist, surrounded by scenes from the life of Christ. Original size

PLATE VIII

13. ZACHARIAS AND THE ANGEL

zacha | riastur | batusest

ZACHARIAS TURBATUS EST (cf. Luke i. 12). On the left the angel advances towards Zacharias who stands behind an altar with his left hand raised.

14. CHRIST AMONGST THE DOCTORS

filiqvid | fecisti | nobissic

FILI QUID FECISTI NOBIS SIC (cf. Luke ii. 48). The virgin advances from the left towards Christ who is seated between two men.

15. CHRIST TEACHING FROM THE BOAT

hicsedens | in navido | cebateos

HIC SEDENS IN NAVI DOCEBAT EOS (cf. Luke v. 3). On the left three figures. On the right Christ in a boat with a disciple. The shore is represented by a vertical wavy line.

16. ST PETER FALLS AT CHRIST'S FEET

petrus | procidit | adgenua | ihu

PETRUS PROCIDIT AD GENUA IESU (cf. Luke v. 8). On the left the lake with a boat on it. On the edge grow small plants. On the right Christ with a disciple on his left in front of whom St Peter lies prostrate.

17. THE RAISING OF THE SON OF THE WIDOW OF NAIN

eccedefunc | tuseffer

ECCE DEFUNCTUS EFFEREBATUR (cf. Luke vii. 12). On the left a city wall from the gate of which emerges a bier carried in front by two men. Upon it lies a man. On the right Christ stretches forward his right hand and touches the head of the corpse.

18. THE CALL OF LEVI

ihsdixit | sequere | me

IESUS DIXIT SEQUERE ME (cf. Luke v. 27). Levi on the left with his right hand raised. On the right Christ with a disciple.

PLATE VIII

CAMBRIDGE, CORPUS CHRISTI COLLEGE MS. 286, f. 129b
Enlarged details, left side

PLATE IX

19. CHRIST AND THE LAWYER

LEGIS | PERITUS | SURREXIT | TEMTANSILLŪ

LEGIS PERITUS SURREXIT TEMTANS ILLUM (cf. Luke x. 25). Christ with a disciple on the left, the lawyer on the right.

20. CHRIST HAILED BY A WOMAN

EXTOLLIT | UOCEMQUAE | DAMMULIER | DETURBAD

EXTOLLIT VOCEM QUAEDAM MULIER DE TURBA DIXIT (cf. Luke xi. 27). On the left a woman accompanied by a bald-headed man. On the right Christ addressing a disciple. The abbreviation 'ᴈ' for 'dixit' should be noted.

21. FOXES HAVE HOLES

IHSDIXIT | UULPESFOS | SAHABENT

IESUS DIXIT VULPES FOSSA HABENT (cf. Luke ix. 58). On the left Christ, with a disciple, raises his right hand. In front of him on the right are three men, the foremost genuflecting. If in fact this scene does illustrate this passage of St Luke, we must assume that in the archetype there was an upper portion of the scene showing the foxes in their holes and the birds in their nests as appears in the twelfth-century English miniature in British Museum, Add. MS. 37472 (I) verso (see M. R. James, 'Four Leaves of an English Psalter' in *Walpole Society*, vol. xxv (1937), pl. iv).

22. THE PARABLE OF THE FIG-TREE

DEFICUL | NEA

DE FICULNEA (cf. Luke xiii. 6). On the left a disciple. Christ in the middle stretches his right hand over a prostrate figure (the keeper of the vineyard?), behind whom grows a tree.

23. THE MIRACLE OF THE DROPSICAL MAN

YDROPI | CUMCURA | UITIHS

YDROPICUM CURAVIT IESUS (cf. Luke xiv. 2). On the left Christ stretches forward his right hand towards a man who is naked except for a cloth. On the right stands a bald-headed man, who is similar to the figure in scene 20. In this case he may be meant to represent one of the Pharisees (see Luke xiv. 3).

24. CHRIST AND ZACHAEUS

ZACHEUS | INARBORE

ZACHEUS IN ARBORE (cf. Luke xix). On the left a disciple; in the middle Christ looking up points with his right hand towards Zachaeus, who stands in a tree on the right. The figures of Christ and Zachaeus should perhaps be compared with the representation of this scene on the doors of the tomb in the fifth-century ivory of the Women at the Sepulchre now in the Civico Museo d'Arte de Castello Sforzesco in Milan (see an excellent photograph reproduced in *Atlantis*, Heft 2 (1949), p. 81).

PLATE IX
CAMBRIDGE, CORPUS CHRISTI COLLEGE MS. 286, f. 129b
Enlarged details, right side

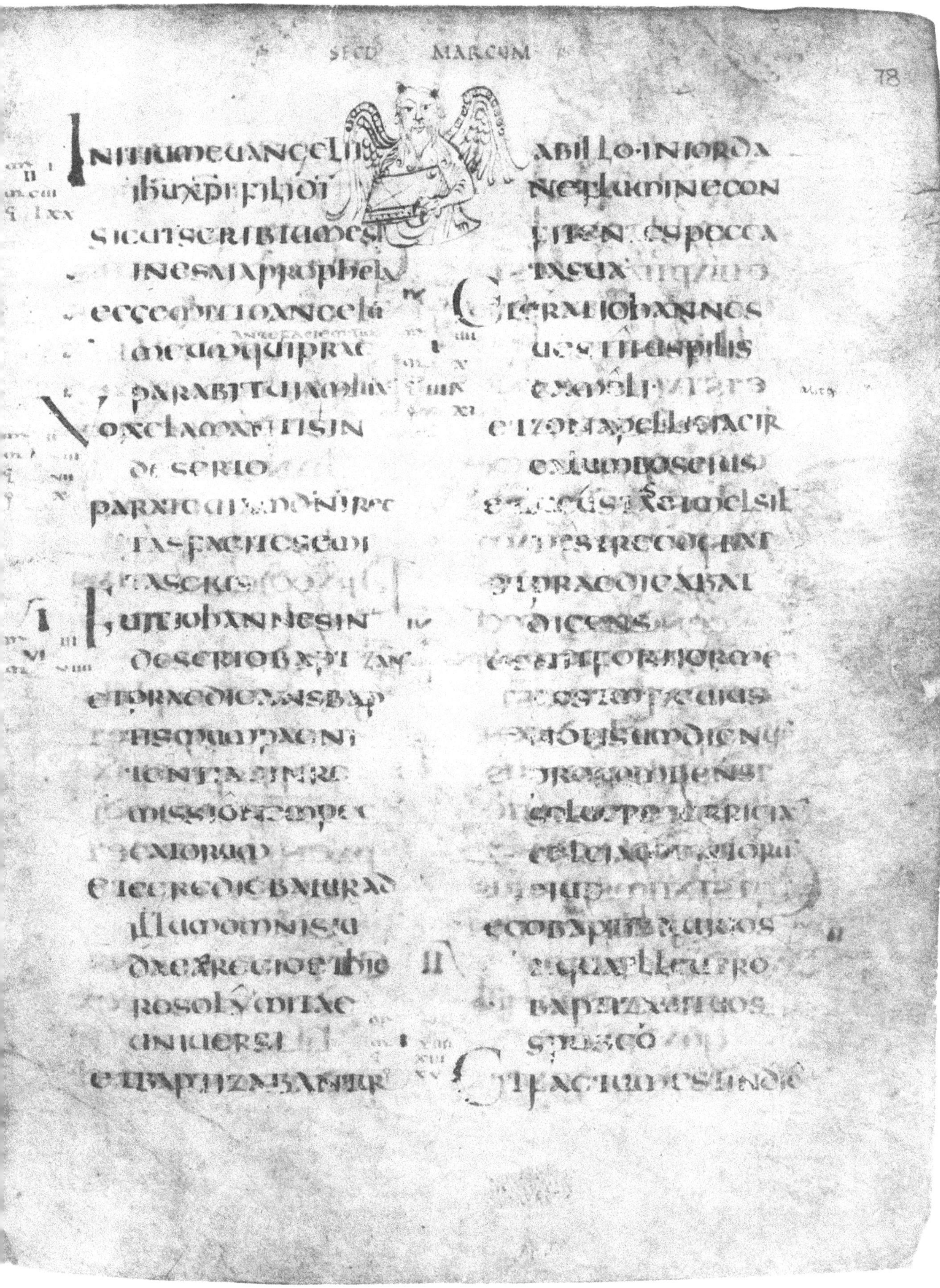

INITIUMEUANGELII
IHUXPIFILIOI
SICUTSCRIBTUMEST
INESAIAPROPHETA
ECCEEGOMITTOANGELU
MEUMANTEQUIPRAE
PARABITUIAMTUAM
UOXCLAMANTISIN
DESERTO
PARATEUIAMDNIREC
TASFACITESEMI
TASEIUS

FUITIOHANNESIN
DESERTOBAPTIZANS
ETPRAEDICANSBAP
TISMUMPAENI
TENTIAEINRE
MISSIONEMPEC
CATORUM
ETEGREDIEBATURAD
ILLUMOMNISIU
DAEAREGIOETHIE
ROSOLYMITAE
UNIUERSI
ETBAPTIZABANTUR

ABILLOINIORDA
NEFLUMINECON
FITENTESPECCA
TASUA
ETERATIOHANNES
UESTITUSPILIS
CAMELIETZONA
ETZONAPELLICIACIR
CALUMBOSEIUS
ETLOCUSTASETMELSIL
UESTREEDEBAT
ETPRAEDICABAT
DICENS
UENITFORTIORME
POSTMEIUSNON
SUMDIGNUS
PROCUMBENSSOL
UERECORRIGIAM
CALCEAMENTORU
EGOBAPTIZAUIUOS
AQUAILLEUERO
BAPTIZABITUOS
SPUSCO
ETFACTUMESTINDIE

PLATE X

CAMBRIDGE, CORPUS CHRISTI COLLEGE MS. 286, f. 78
The beginning of St Mark's Gospel. Original size

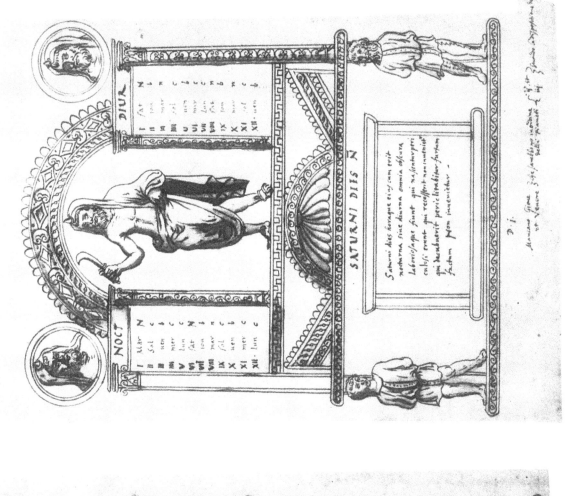

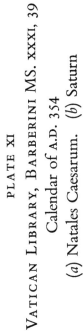

PLATE XI

VATICAN LIBRARY, BARBERINI MS. XXXI, 39

Calendar of A.D. 354

(a) Natales Caesarum. (b) Saturn

PLATE XII

(a) KARLSRUHE, LANDESMUSEUM, Mithras Stele

(b) TUNIS, MUSEO DEL BARDO, Virgil between Clio and Melpomene. Mosaic from Susa, N. Africa, second century A.D.

PLATE XIII

MILAN, DUOMO, TREASURY. Ivory diptych, fifth century
(a) Symbols of St Matthew and St Luke, with the Nativity of Christ
(b) Symbols of St Mark and St John, with the Adoration of the Magi

PLATE XIV

(*a*) CAMBRIDGE, CORPUS CHRISTI COLLEGE MS. 286, f. 129b
St Luke's symbol. Original size

(*b*) BRITISH MUSEUM, ROYAL MS. IE. VI, f. 43
St Luke's symbol

PLATE XV

STOCKHOLM, ROYAL LIBRARY, Codex Aureus, MS. A. 135

Reduced. (*a*) St Matthew; (*b*) St John

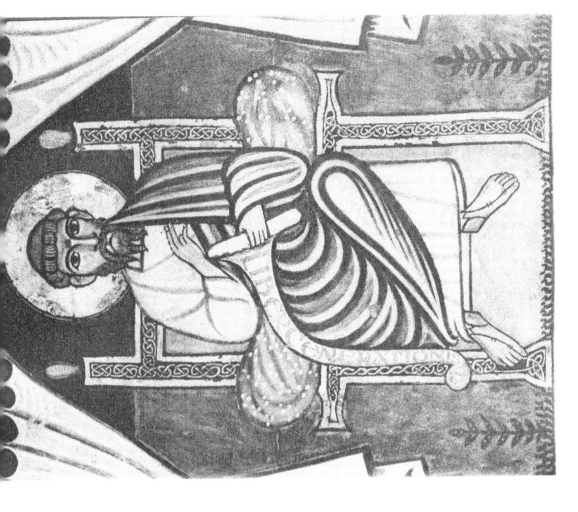

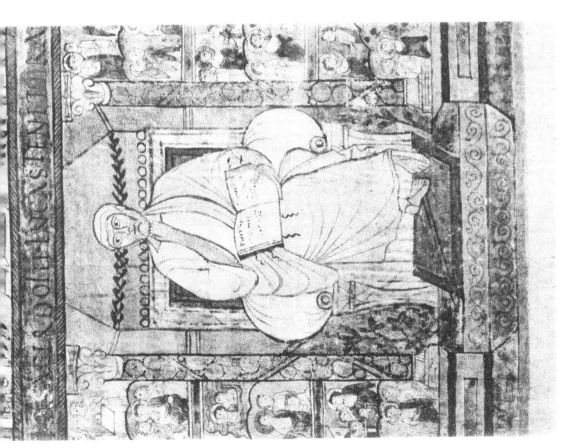

PLATE XVI

(a) Cambridge, Corpus Christi College MS. 286, f. 129b
St Luke. Detail, original size

(b) Stockholm, Royal Library, Codex Aureus, MS. A. 135
St Matthew. Detail, original size

PLATE XVII
CAMBRIDGE, UNIVERSITY LIBRARY, MS. Ll. I. 10, f. 12b (the Book of Cerne)
St Mark. Original size

PLATE XVIII

CAMBRIDGE, UNIVERSITY LIBRARY, MS. Ll. i. 10, f. 21 b (the Book of Cerne)
St Luke. Original size

PLATE XIX

CAMBRIDGE, UNIVERSITY LIBRARY, MS. Ll. 1. 10, f. 31 b (the Book of Cerne)
St John. Original size

www.ingramcontent.com/pod-product-compliance
Ingram Content Group UK Ltd.
Pitfield, Milton Keynes, MK11 3LW, UK
UKHW052113280225
455719UK00013B/448